IS LOOKING
FOR THOSE...

WHO WILL STAND WITH HIM
WHO ARE AVAILABLE
WHO WILL STAND IN THE GAP
WHO WILL LISTEN
WHO HAVE A SINGLE EYE
WHO BEAR HIS IMAGE

DEVERN FROMKE

Cover Illustration: Creation and Copyright © 2007 Steve Cannon

Published by SHARPER FOCUS PUBLISHING division of
SURE FOUNDATION CRT
5671 Polk Drive
Noblesville, IN 46062
www.FromkeBooks.com

Distributed by BOOK DEPOT
11298 Old Paths Lane
Shoals, Indiana 47581-7234

Scripture quotations noted LB are from *THE LIVING BIBLE*. Copyright 1971 by Tyndale House Publishing. Wheaton, IL. Used by permission.

Scripture quotations noted Msg -*THE MESSAGE,* Eugene Peterson. Copyright 1993, 1994, 1995, 1996 and 2000. Used by permission of NavPress Publishing Group. All rights reserved.

Scripture quotations noted NASB from the *NEW AMERICAN STANDARD BIBLE*. Copyright 1960, 1962, 1963, 1977 by The Lockman Foundation. Used by permission.

Scripture quotations noted NCV are from *THE HOLY BIBLE, NEW CENTURY VERSION*. Copyright 1987, 1988, and 1991 by Word Publishing, a division of Thomas Nelson, Inc. Used by permission.

Scripture quotations noted NEB are from *THE NEW ENGLISH BIBLE*. Cambridge: At the University Press, 1972.

Scripture quotations noted NIV are from the *HOLY BIBLE New International Version*. Copyright 1973, 1978, and 1984 International Bible Society. Used by permission.

Scripture quotations noted NKJV from the *NEW KING JAMES VERSION*. Copyright 1979, 1980, 1982 by Thomas Nelson, Inc. Used by permission.

Scripture quotations noted Phil are from *THE HOLY BIBLE, PHILLIPS VERSION BIBLE*. Used by permission of TouchStone Publishing House, New York, NY 10020. All rights reserved.

CONTENTS

INTRODUCTION

WHAT DO WE MEAN BY FOCUS? Let me explain with this quote from Charles Cowman:

> The human eye is so constituted that a sailor standing night-lookout watch at sea, can see a dim object more clearly by focusing on a point a little to one side of it, than by staring directly at it. In a similar manner, your spiritual vision is designed so that you can see God's will for you, not by concentrating on it, but by looking at Him.

This can be an important correction for those who become focused on knowing God's will. We should never let seeking God's will become a substitute for God Himself. When we are rightly occupied with our Father/God, we shall find that knowing His will falls into its rightful place. Walking "in His light, we shall see light."

You will discover that the primary message of each focus manual is to keep you occupied with the Lord. You can be sure

He is so delighted with this choice that He will order your footsteps in the UNFOLDING OF HIS WILL.

One of the great spiritual giants who had caught the attention of the world, whispered on his deathbed, "Perhaps the greatest thing I have learned in my lifetime is my ACCOUNTABILITY TO GOD."

That summary of his learning so caught my attention that (more than forty years ago) I copied his words into the back page of my study Bible. Then, as my own life-focus I added, "My availability, my adjustability, and my accountability will be my constant focus—a life seeking to be well-pleasing to Him."

If you will read and meditate on these lessons day by day— rather than racing through them to finish the book—we will be pleased, and we believe you will receive much greater value in your daily fellowship with Him.

Remember we are family! We seek for your spiritual welfare as we meet you daily…

AT HIS THRONE OF GRACE,
DeVern & Ruth

Our Father is looking for those who will seek Him early in the morning. Have you noticed that the more important people are in their position, the more likely they are to find a solitary place where they can pray and meditate? Consider some busy people who save time in getting prepared for the day by...

PUTTING HIM FIRST

DR. BEN CARSON, chief of pediatric neurosurgery at John Hopkins Children's Center found time each morning for prayer and reading from the book of Proverbs. He said, "During the day, if I encounter a frustrating situation, I think back to one of the verses that I had read that morning. How often God had prepared a verse for that day."

In 1946, I met Dr. H. J. Ockenga when he visited the campus of Seattle Pacific University. After the morning chapel address he shared several significant things from his personal life. At that time he was the president of the National Association of Evangelicals and later moved on to found Fuller Theological Seminary, becoming its first president. He had been the senior pastor at Park Street Church in Boston and later became president of Gordon College.

With all these positions there was a quality and spiritual tone that set him apart. He explained to us, "I have always been very busy, but here is my secret—I keep a prayer list...and write a brief summary of the petition, number it and date it. When it is answered, I write "answered" across it. It is in leaving things with God that I am released from anxiety. Therefore I need not worry about it." When asked how he found time to pray, he continued, "I exercise, shave and bathe. Then I pray until breakfast—picking up where I left off on my prayer list. I've had this prayer habit from the time I went to college."

President Lincoln recognized his need. A gentleman having an appointment to meet the President arrived a quarter of an hour early. While waiting for the appointed time he heard in the next room a voice as if in grave conversation. He asked the attendant standing by, "Who is talking in the next room?"

"Oh, it is the President, sir."

"Is anybody with him?" the gentleman inquired. "Is that his habit so early in the morning?"

"Yes, sir, he spends every morning from 4:00 to 5:00 reading the Bible and praying."

Consider the mighty voice which challenged the religious system of Europe and ignited the reformation. Martin Luther once confided, "I am so busy that if I do not spend two or three hours each day in prayer, I could not get through the day."

When asked about the amazing growth of his ministry, Yonggi Cho answered, "How can I pray a minimum of three hours every day and still pastor one of the largest churches in the world with a congregation of over 400,000, plus travel every month to church growth conferences? The key is setting up my priorities. By praying, I can save many hours—by having my mind renewed and prepared with answers almost before questions are asked. God shows me potential problems in our ministry so I can apply preventative spiritual solutions. Frankly, I cannot afford to skip even an hour of prayer time."

PONDER THIS PRINCIPLE: C. S. Lewis wrote, "If God had granted all the silly prayers I've made in my life, where would I be now?" This means that much of our time in His presence should be waiting—listening to hear His voice. Only then can we know how to pray according to His will—and have the confidence He will answer.

GOD'S WORD IS CLEAR: ...*They that wait upon the Lord shall renew their strength...* (Isa. 40:31 KJV)

...men have not heard...neither hath the eye seen...what (God) hath prepared for him that waiteth for him (Isa. 64:4 KJV)

...Our soul waits for the Lord... (Psa. 33:20 NKJV)

Truly my soul silently waits for God; from Him comes my salvation. (Psa. 62:1 NKJV)

My soul, wait thou only upon God; for my expectation is from him. (Psa. 62:5 KJV)

WE PRAY: Father, we can only say that we must have more than desire; we must have your enablement to keep this a priority every day.

Focus for Praying

He learned to stand with God in crisis times; this explains the effective ministry of John Paton, missionary to the New Hebrides Islands. God is always looking for those who will recognize Him as their only Source in facing...

THE CHALLENGE

WHEN John Paton arrived in this mission area the people were naked savages who lived in a state of debauchery. His first great challenge was in getting the people to believe he had a message from God. This burden weighed heavily so he kept his heart tuned to hear God's voice. As he waited, he claimed some opportunity for God to demonstrate.

One day the water supply ran out on the island because of lack of rain. After praying for God's help, Paton proceeded to dig a well. Since the people had never seen a well, it was difficult when he told the chief that he believed God would give them rain from the hole in the ground. The only fresh water the natives had was caught when it rained.

When Paton made this statement, great excitement prevailed. The chief and others declared that if Paton could bring rain from the hole in the ground, his must be the true God.

Finally by digging to some depth, the missionary found a spring of fresh water. The effect upon the people was wonderful. The old chief asked the privilege of preaching a sermon at the well in the Sunday services. This he did, emphasizing his earnest appeal by excitedly swinging his tomahawk. In the midst of his sermon he cried, "People of Aniwa, the world has turned upside down since the Word of Jehovah is come to this land. Who ever expected to see rain come up through the earth? From this day I must worship Him who has opened up for us this well, and who fills it with rain from below."

During the week following this remarkable sermon, great heaps of idols were burned in front of Paton's house. This amazing power of the gospel was demonstrated many times during Paton's years of ministry.

When he attempted to translate the Scriptures he could find no term for "faith" or "believe" in their language. He struggled and searched until one day when a tired Christian dropped into a lounging chair in his study. As he dropped he sighed, "Oh how good it is to lean your whole weight on the chair." Immediately Paton knew that was what he had been looking for, prompting this translation, *"God so loved the world that He gave His only begotten Son that whosoever believed (leaned his whole weight) on Him should not perish but have everlasting life."*

Is it too much to expect? If we are truly in partnership with Him, God will arrange circumstances to perform a miracle of "water from a hole"—or to help us find the right word for "believe."

Many other incidents in the life of John G. Paton reveal how he stood with God. When three witch doctors claimed they had the power to cause his death, they publicly announced their intentions to kill him before the next Sunday by using sorcery. To carry out their threat, they said they needed some food he had partially eaten. So Paton asked for three plums. He took a bite out of each and then gave them to the men who were plotting his death.

On Sunday, the missionary entered the village with a smile on his face and a spring in his step. The people looked at each other in amazement, thinking it could not possibly be Paton.

The failure in their demonstration had put them to shame. The "sacred men" admitted that they had tried by their incantations to kill him. When asked why they had failed, they replied that the missionary was a sacred man like themselves, but they realized his God was stronger than theirs. Paton's influence grew, and soon he had the joy of leading more of these villagers to the Lord.

PONDER THIS PRINCIPLE: We cannot move God to stand with us in our need. Only when we move over to stand with Him for His purposes, can we face the subtle challenge from the Enemy.

GOD'S WORD IS CLEAR: ...*He who is in you, is greater than he who is in the world.* (1 John 4:4 NKJV) Satan uses his great intelligence and power to try to defeat God's servants. But the indwelling Holy Spirit enables the believer to overcome any challenge.

WE PRAY: Father, help us to keep our eyes focused on You, so we will be VICTORS instead of victims.

Focus for Praying

_____

_____

_____

_____

_____

_____

_____

_____

_____

_____

_____

_____

_____

_____

_____

_____

_____

_____

_____

_____

_____

A mother shares the following: For several years I was perplexed. I was beseeching God for help in dealing with my wayward son. We were a leading family in our church and it was most embarrassing for us. In spite of all my praying he seemed to increase his rebellion and reckless escapades. Then I discovered where I was...

WRONG IN MY PRAYING

A GREAT change came one night when I discovered what it would mean to be identified with Him in a new position. Suddenly I realized how fleshly mother-ties had colored all my praying. I saw that actually I was not so much concerned for God as for my son—and how his behavior affected me.

I saw how, as a typical mother with her outspread protective wings I was seeking to shield my son from harm and danger, even shield him from anything God might need to allow to awaken him. I had always identified more with my son than with God.

Then, in His own gentle way, He took the cross as His scissors. He asked for permission to cut these fleshly ties that I might be released from standing with my son. It meant taking a big move away from him over into the heart of God. I saw how this new identification might involve cost to me. If I began praying from this new position, I should be willing for any course necessary to bring my boy to God.

14

I did give Him permission! Immediately I sensed that my relationship with my son seemed different. The next night when he was leaving to go out for a time with his friends, I called him aside.

"Son, I have something important to tell you. I want you to know that as your mother, I love you, even more than I have been able to show. But I am no longer praying that God will spare you from harm when you race with the boys. I am no longer standing with you, beseeching God in your behalf! From now on I am standing with God for His purpose and plan in your life. In His stead I beseech you to turn from your wild reckless ways and yield to God."

The boy pretended he was unconcerned and left the house with the typical teenage attitude of "so what—who cares." But strangely he could not get away from his mother's haunting words. They penetrated as words never had before. Mother seemed to speak with such new authority. He knew there was something different in her eyes. Did she really love God more than him? He tried to enjoy his reckless times with the gang, but his mother's words and look kept haunting him.

One whole month passed. Mother was different! She didn't nag, didn't scold. She simply walked with her new confidence that God was at work. And He was!

Although the details are omitted, it was only a short time before a crisis brought that son to know God for Himself, not merely for himself. For many years now he has been a veteran soldier of the cross on the mission field. It all happened because a mother had learned the secret of STANDING WITH GOD....

Would you believe this mother told me the above story more than thirty years ago? My wife and I have experienced this personally, and we have observed many parents who took the same move to stand with God.

PONDER THIS PRINCIPLE: There is a big difference between our standing with God beseeching man to be reconciled, and our standing with man beseeching God to save. Only as we allow God to cut our soul-ties (emotional bondage) can we truly realize how rebellion touches His heart.

GOD'S WORD IS CLEAR: We have Paul's own admonition, *...Seeing we have this ministry, (of standing with God) as we have received mercy, we faint not. We have renounced the hidden things of dishonesty...* (2 Cor. 4:1, 2 KJV)

WE PRAY: Father, we know there are scores of your children who are still entangled in their emotional ties with family and friends. They are so tangled they cannot pray for them effectively. They are still inclined by sympathy for the lost to blame God because He seems so slow in working...until they make this important move.

Focus for Praying

When we pray, supplication is seeking to know the mind of God, so we are praying TOWARD the will of God. By contrast authoritative praying is FROM the will of God. We may speak boldly because we are sure what the will of God is. As an example of authoritative praying consider how…

LUTHER WAS EXCEEDINGLY BOLD

TO SOME it may seem extremely audacious to make such a bold command, even in such circumstances. Yet through the years God has often sought and found a man who would stand with Him—and in authority exercise some kingdom rights.

In 1540 Martin Luther's good friend, Myconius, became deathly ill. Along with others, Myconius expected he would die within a short time. One night he wrote with his trembling hand a farewell to Luther, whom he loved very much.

When Luther received the letter, he immediately sent back the following reply. "I command thee in the name of God to live because I have need of thee in the work of reforming the church. The Lord will never let me hear that thou art dead, but will permit thee to survive me. For this I am praying. This is my will, and may THY will be done, because I seek only to glorify the name of God."

Myconius had already lost the faculty of speech when Luther's letter came. But in a short time he was well again, and actually some years later survived Luther by two months.

How shall we explain this unusual boldness of Luther? You have, no doubt, heard individuals boldly command God to perform some miracle for His glory. For most of us, it is hard to accept the creature commanding His Creator!

Many years ago the message in a booklet written by a veteran missionary urged folk to *"command ye Me according to the work of My hands."* He insisted that under certain circumstances it was appropriate and necessary to use authoritative praying to deal with the Enemy and claim lost ground for God. Using this approach we saw victory come in several crises when the Enemy was forced to yield ground.

Because we were standing with God—acting on His behalf—it was necessary to use the Name of Jesus to win victory. However, we soon came to recognize that this verse in Isaiah 45:11 is actually a question God is asking us, not a promise that He will respond to our initiative.

Thus God, the Holy of Israel, Israel's Maker, says:
Do you question who or what I'm making?
Are you telling me what I can or cannot do? (Msg)

How shall we interpret this verse? Is it our privilege? Or is it mere presumption—that God will respond when we claim a victory *"according to the work of My hands?"*

Once again, we need to understand; it is clearly a matter of discernment. Too often it is man presuming to command God—and that is dangerous. But, we believe Luther was not acting on his own. If we can receive it, God is seeking to give on-the-job-training in overcoming the forces hostile to His purpose. Luther could look into God's heart and claim, "God you know I am not pleading for personal advantage, nor trying to avoid hardship—I am only standing with You that Your full purpose may be accomplished—and Thy name be glorified."

Would you move down in Isaiah 45 to verse 14 and consider, *The workers of Egypt, the merchants of Ethiopia, and those statuesque Sabeans...will all come over to you—all yours, Docile in chains, they'll follow you, Hands folded in reverence, praying before you:*
Amazing! God is with you!
There is no other God—none. (Isa. 45:14 Msg)
Clearly, You are a God who works behind the scenes.

PONDER THIS PRINCIPLE: The boldness of the flesh disgusts—but the boldness of the Spirit disarms. God will honor those who honor Him; He will vindicate your boldness, whether you are presumptive...or acting in DIVINE PRIVILEGE.

GOD'S WORD: In that great hour of testing our Lord Jesus boldly announced, *...Not My will, but Thine, be done* (Luke 22:42 KJV)

WE PRAY: Father what else can we say—Thy will be done!

Focus for Praying

Very often God allows us to fill a need, even though we cannot understand at that moment. We simply offer ourselves to Him to be available, adjustable and accountable. How much this next incident reveals the importance of offering love when...

THERE IS NO ONE ELSE

A NURSE took the tired, anxious serviceman to the bedside of an elderly man and announced, "Your son is here." She had to repeat the words several times before the patient's eyes opened. Heavily sedated because of the pain from his heart attack, he dimly saw the young uniformed Marine standing outside the oxygen tent. He reached out his hand. The Marine wrapped his toughened fingers around the old man's limp ones, squeezing a message of love and encouragement.

The nurse waited, and then brought a chair so the Marine could sit beside the bed. All through the night the young Marine sat there in the dimly lighted ward, holding the old man's hand and offering words of love and strength.

Occasionally, the nurse suggested that he move away and rest awhile, but he refused. Whenever the nurse came into the ward, the Marine was oblivious of her and of the night noises—the clanking of the oxygen tank, the laughter of the night staff members exchanging greetings, the cries and moans of the other patients. Now and then she heard him say a few gentle words. The dying man said nothing, only held tightly to his son all through the night.

Along toward dawn the old man took his last breath. There was no struggle, only a peaceful passing away. The Marine released the now lifeless hand he had been holding and went to tell the nurse. He observed her quietly as she fulfilled her duties.

Finally, she returned. She started to offer words of sympathy, but the Marine interrupted her. "Who was that man?" he asked.

The nurse was startled, "He was your father," she answered.

"No, he wasn't," the Marine replied. "I never saw him before in my life."

"Then why didn't you say something when I took you to him?"

"I knew right away there had been a mistake, but I also knew he needed his son, and his son just wasn't here. When I realized that he was too sick to tell whether or not I was his son—knowing how much he needed me—I stayed."

What a privilege for the Marine to be there in this time of need. But I wondered what the dying man needed most: was it his son, or THE SON? Was he prepared to meet God? Had he ever placed his trust in Christ as His Savior? There is such a great difference between meeting his temporal need or his eternal need. We do not even know whether the Marine was a believer and could lead him to Christ. But just now, we do not need to know!

PONDER THIS PRINCIPLE: Surely the most important issue is not our knowing, but our obedience to God. Often we try to understand so we can choose our obedience. Instead of immediately obeying the Lord of Life—the one condition upon which He can help—we allow our unenlightened minds to intrude before we obey. This is a universal failure among His children. Father is LOOKING FOR THOSE WHO WILL HEAR AND OBEY.

GOD'S WORD IS CLEAR: Samuel the prophet warned, *...It is better to obey than to sacrifice. It is better to listen to God than to offer the fat of sheep.* (1 Sam. 15:22 NCV). King Saul had defeated the Amalekites in battle and should have utterly destroyed the animals. But his reasoning took over, "What a terrible waste to just kill them! Since God is delighted in our sacrificing to Him—why not offer them in sacrifice?" God was not pleased.

WE PRAY: Father, we are often guilty of sparing something in our lives that seems "so good!" Keep us from this temptation of coming short of full obedience. Help us first of all to yield our body as a "living sacrifice" to You.

Focus for Praying

Why does it take an emergency for God to get our attention? Simple! We are too preoccupied with "doing our own thing." Be sure of this—if we belong to Him, He is looking for some crisis that will press us to go beyond praying and to...

CRY OUT FOR HELP

A MOTHER awakened out of a sound sleep, rolling and tossing until finally she realized God was calling her to prayer. She had no knowledge that anything was wrong. Could it be that one of her children needed help, although they were all grown and away? With strong groanings in the spirit she interceded until finally rest came.

Several months later when her son returned from the service, he told how their submarine became stranded on the bottom of the ocean. The mechanics tried in vain to repair the engines, which remained dead. The commander summoned the crew and explained their desperate plight. It was a terrible moment of reckoning. They had nothing to look forward to but a watery grave—unless someone could get help from God.

Without hesitancy this son offered to pray. He cried out to God while every subdued sailor waited. Having finished, he turned with a start of elation. "I have an impression, Sir; would you allow me to try something in the engine room?" Permission was granted. He did! To their utter amazement the engines started. Every man knew God had intervened, and they had been rescued from a watery grave.

Now some months later mother and son reckoned the time; it was during those very hours the mother had interceded that night before God.

These past years, our nation has been awakened to the power of crying out to God. The seminar ministry of Bill Gothard and his book present testimonies of many who have experienced God's great deliverance.

PONDER THIS PRINCIPLE: While God is ever-present waiting to help His children, His Father-heart knows the right timing—when our desperation causes us to want Him for Himself...not just for ourselves.

GOD'S WORD: We recall how another victim, Jonah, in the belly of a great fish called out in desperation:

...I cried by reason of my affliction unto the Lord and He heard me.... I will pay that which I have vowed, Salvation is of the Lord. And the Lord spake unto the fish, and it vomited out Jonah upon dry land. (Jonah 2:2, 9-10 KJV)

WE PRAY: Father, forgive us for coming to You only when we are desperate. In the past we have sought Your hand for help. Now, we will seek Your face—to enjoy fellowship with You.

Focus for Praying

How available are we for divine encounters? Each morning we ask the Lord to use us as His witness, and yet do we miss opportunities daily because...? We will consider several reasons. Just listen to this account of one who was...

INSTANT IN SEASON

I RECALL this story of one of God's servants who boarded a plane. He had just finished a very exhausting week and was looking forward to some quiet time relaxing during the flight.

But God had other plans. In his row, the window seat was occupied by a (clearly) limited young lad and between them in the middle seat was an obviously successful businessman who immediately opened his laptop computer to do some work.

They were hardly off the runway, when the young lad turned to the middle businessman and asked, "Sir, do you brush your teeth?"

There was a moment of uncomfortable silence...until the man graciously answered, "Yes, I do...every morning...why do you ask?"

"Well, your teeth will fall out if you don't," was the lad's quick response.

A few moments passed, and the next question came... "Do you fly in airplanes very much?"

Though the businessman clearly disliked being interrupted, he again courteously replied, "Yes, I do fly every
week."

The boy seemed satisfied and waited several minutes
before asking his next question, "Sir, do you go to church?"
The question from the lad next to the window really needed
an answer.

So the man carefully answered, "Yes, I go to church
sometimes, but may I ask why you are so interested?"

The servant of God who had quietly listened to their
conversation had not become involved, but he pondered what
the lad's answer might be. Then it came—with much
emphasis, "Well, it isn't enough to go to church, you really
need to love Jesus. I hope you do...would you ask the man
next to you if he loves Jesus?"

What a strained silence—and awkward moment—as the
business man turned and whispered, "I think you had better
do that."

So the young lad leaned over to get the attention of the
servant of God (who had overheard the entire episode with
much delight)... "Sir, do you love Jesus?"

The servant of God recognized his opportunity, so he was
quick to respond, as his broad smile met the face of the
businessman. "Yes, I do love Him—very much; in fact, He is
my real purpose for living."

It was in that moment he realized God had maneuvered this divine encounter. Without hesitation, the businessman admitted that this unusual question was one he could not answer but that had really troubled him for months. For the next hour he opened his heart and the servant of God was keenly aware that God had placed him in the right seat at the right time. Not only were many deep questions answered, but that seeking businessman was urged to trust Christ as his personal Lord and Savior...without delay. Eternity will reveal what happened!

I am uncertain as to the further details of this encounter, but it serves to demonstrate: God will help us to fill the deep need in another—if we live expectantly—and quietly wait for Him to open doors.

If you seek to be a God-pleaser more than a man-pleaser, God can arrange circumstances. Usually when we dare to follow the immediate impulse of the Holy Spirit we will be used by God; but if we start to analyze the situation or personal consequences we will squirm out of becoming available. I know—and have recognized later, that I missed an opportunity.

PONDER THIS PRINCIPLE: The eyes of the Lord look everywhere to find expectant, humble, willing vessels whom He can use. The good news is this: almost every day we discover how God is using folk to transform lives by their simple obedience.

GOD'S WORD IS CLEAR: *...be instant in season, out of season...do the work of an evangelist, make full proof of thy ministry...* (2 Tim. 4:2, 5 KJV). We realize that Timothy was not an evangelist, yet Paul was encouraging him to be available for this work.

WE PRAY: Lord, would You please keep me in such intimate fellowship with You that I am expectant...that I will take the low place...that I am drawing from Your supply daily? Today I am praying that I will become totally available to You.

Focus for Praying

_____

_____

_____

_____

_____

_____

_____

_____

_____

_____

_____

_____

_____

_____

_____

In the Bible we read that God is constantly watching over His children. But it is good that we should remind Him what He has promised. Take a quick look through your concordance and consider how often the word remember is used. In this incident we are alerted to see the importance of being...

CONTINUALLY REMINDING HIM

DIANE, a young university student, was home for the summer. She had gone to visit some friends one evening and time passed quickly as each shared their spiritual experiences of the past year. Staying longer than she'd planned, Diane ended up walking home alone in the dark.

It was a small town and her home was only a few blocks away, so Diane wasn't afraid. As she walked along under the tall elm trees, she asked God to keep her safe from harm and danger. When she reached the alley—a short cut to her house—Diane decided to take it. However, halfway down the alley she noticed a man standing at the end as though he were waiting for her. She became uneasy and began to pray earnestly, seeking God's protection. Instantly, a comforting feeling of quietness and security wrapped around her; she felt as though someone was walking with her.

When she reached the end of the alley, she walked right past the man and arrived home safely. The following day, a newspaper article alerted Diane to the fact that a young girl had been raped in the same alley just twenty minutes after she had been there. Feeling overwhelmed by this tragedy and knowing that it could have been her, she began to weep.

Thanking the Lord for her safety, she went to the police station hoping to be of some help to this young woman. When she told them her story, the police asked if she would be willing to look at a lineup and attempt to identify the perpetrator. She agreed and immediately pointed out the man she had passed in the alley the night before. When the man learned he had been recognized, he immediately broke down and confessed.

The officer thanked Diane for her bravery and asked if there was anything they could do for her. She requested that they question the man as to why he had not assaulted her. The attacker's answer? "Because she wasn't alone. She had two tall men walking on either side of her."

PONDER THIS PRINCIPLE: We have previously indicated that God has given us countless promises that we do not walk alone and we need not be fearful. Someone has counted all the "fear not's" in God's word and found there are 365...one for each day of the year. So, if His eye is upon us—we are assured we do not walk alone. Yet I am convinced it is our part to be His rememberer.

GOD'S WORD IS CLEAR: Perhaps the first verse that comes to mind is one from that favorite 23rd Psalm. *Yea, though I walk through the valley of the shadow of death, I will fear no evil: for thou art with me; thy rod and thy staff they comfort me.* (vs. 4 KJV)

WE PRAY: Father, I have been so thankful You taught me to PRAY BACK Your word to You. I find such comfort and strength—for I am participating with the "elders of the ages" who have gone before.

Focus for Praying

_____

_____

_____

_____

_____

_____

_____

_____

_____

_____

_____

_____

_____

_____

_____

_____

_____

That God takes special care for those who are on assignment is evident from this most unusual intervention. We know that God is continually looking for an intercessor who will stand in the gap. Because He found one, we have this…

MIRACLE IN THE DESERT

LATE one night I was walking home along a road in the Middle East, after a missionary meeting. The air was still, and I was enjoying some much needed private time with the Lord.

Suddenly, a group of eight men in white turbans jumped out from behind a low wall. Encircling me, they blocked my path on the narrow dirt road. I looked around for help, but no one was in view or earshot. I don't think I could have screamed for help anyway. My vocal cords, along with the rest of me, were paralyzed with fear. I wish I could say I was a woman of great faith and power. The truth is, I was scared.

Reality hit me full force. These men could have cared less that I was a missionary in their country. I was a fair-skinned, blue-eyed, foreign, blond woman—not a very good thing to be on a dark, lonely road. With arms folded across their chests, legs slightly spread and firmly planted, these men leered at me. I searched one face after another for mercy. They stared back, unmoving.

A thought blasted into my mind, "This isn't fair! God has further plans for my life; I can't die now." Then God's Word welled up inside of me—*"Greater is He who is in you than he who is in the world. No weapon formed against you shall prosper. God's Word never fails."* Immobilizing fear was cast out, replaced with a flood of righteous anger.

"Out of my way! Please!" I said, staring at the man who seemed to be the leader.

Nothing happened. He just smiled crudely at me and chuckled. The others joined in. Their laughter was enough to cause the hairs on my arms to stand straight up. Then it dawned on me; they didn't understand English. I was trying to think of another way to communicate when I remembered the Name that knows no language barriers. I pointed my finger right in the ringleader's face.

"In the name of Jesus, let me go through," I commanded him.

He looked around sheepishly at his companions, laughed nervously, and smiled ever so slightly at me. I smiled back. Then bent down at the waist with his right arm extended, he made a wide, sweeping bow, motioning me by him. I squeezed in between him and the man next to him and began to walk away. My heart was screaming *"Run!"* But I knew that if I did, they would surely come after me. When I was a distance away, curiosity overcame me, and I glanced back over my shoulder.

A strange sight greeted my eyes. Not one of the men had moved an inch! Their arms were still crossed on their chests, and their legs stood in the same position. They were looking at each other, but weren't speaking. I sensed they hadn't moved because they couldn't. I imagined angels with iron grips were holding them in place. I continued to walk slowly to the nearest turn in the road. Finally, after what seemed like an eternity, I made it around the corner. Then I ran for my life!

"Thank you, Father," I whispered, shaking all over.

By the time a month had passed, I'd almost forgotten about the incident. Then I received a letter from my friend in the States. She'd been awakened one night with a vision in which I walked along a road alone. Quite unexpectedly, several tall, concrete-like pillars encircled me. Sensing I was in great danger, my friend began to intercede on my behalf. She fervently repeated those same verses, *"Greater is He who is in you than he who is in the world. No weapon formed against you shall prosper."* As she continued praying, a shaft of light hit one of the pillars, toppling it, and I walked through the shaft of light to safety.

She wrote me at once to find out what might have happened that night. When I read the letter, I was stunned! Her prayer had taken place the same night I'd faced the turbaned men. Praise and thanksgiving again filled my heart as I recalled that miraculous intervention of the Lord.

PONDER THIS PRINCIPLE: No matter how noble their cause, when folk go out on their own...merely because they answer a call...they are on their own. But when they are sent forth by the Lord on a special assignment, God will grant his special protection.

GOD'S WORD IS CLEAR: We read in Acts 13 when Barnabas and Paul were commissioned, *As they ministered to the Lord...the Holy Ghost said, Separate me Barnabas and Saul for the work whereunto I have called them...So they, being sent forth by the Holy Ghost...* (Acts 13:2, 4 KJV) Note there is first a CALLING...then a SENDING.

WE PRAY: Father, we know You are the one who calls us according to Your purpose, but you also send forth those who are duly prepared for the work. Please forgive us for rushing folk out who are merely called, but not yet spiritually prepared for sending.

CHRISTIAN HERALD: "On a Road in the Middle East" by Deborah Strong, in Touching the Heart of God, ed. Leonard E. LeSourd, @1990 (Chosen Books, Fleming H. Revell Co.). Used by permission (©The Breakthrough Intercessor, vol.8, no.6).

Focus for Praying

_____

_____

_____

_____

_____

_____

_____

We have been discovering how God protects those who are on special assignment for Him. This is our assurance that He will intervene in a time of danger because He has already alerted someone to stand in the gap. It is amazing how He will override our ignorance before we understand this rule of the jungle...

DON'T PARK IN A TRAFFIC ZONE

ONE AFTERNOON in the game-infested area of East Africa a missionary family was traveling toward a tribe of people who had never heard the gospel. Quite suddenly, they were drenched by a rain storm, and hastily set up camp for the night. The father tells the following story:

With supper finished, we retired for the night. The children were already asleep when we were disturbed by a spotted hyena. It seemed he was attempting to raid our meager food supply. Quickly, I ran out into the rain and, with a shout and hurled stick, frightened him out of camp.

I hoped things would settle down for the night. But about that time, out of the distance came the roar of a lion. We had not been in jungle country long and were not yet acquainted with the ways of its king. We lay in our beds fearful that the lion was coming our way; waiting through the long intervals between roars, we tried to determine if he was approaching.

Finally exhaustion ruled and we slipped off to sleep, never knowing which way he went that night.

About fifteen minutes before midnight, we were suddenly awakened by the quaking ground, causing our tent to surge—a strange rising and falling under and around us—accompanied in perfect rhythm by a "swish, swish" sound as though some large animal were walking through the tall, wet elephant grass. We knew that rhinos, as well as elephants and lions, were numerous in the area. I surmised that a large rhino was approaching. Knowing that it might charge through our tent killing us all, I slipped quietly from my cot, lifted my rifle, and edged through the tent flaps. Seeing nothing directly in front of me, I peeked around the corner gripping the trigger in expectation of meeting the large brute nearby.

But to my amazement, just twenty-three steps away stood fifteen elephants. They had been traveling single file, head to tail. Seeing our camp, they had stopped. But now, though I had been as quiet and as cautious as possible, they had undoubtedly seen me. Immediately, their trunks trumpeted as is customary before elephants stampede.

My first thought was to fire, but good judgment checked me. For I knew that even if I were to fire every shot in the magazine, there would still be enough elephants left to utterly destroy our camp. Rather, I stepped back. Unintentionally, I bumped the table on which were stacked our tin cooking and eating utensils. To my horror, the table tipped over, spilling the pans with a loud clatter.

I thought for a moment that all was ended. But to my amazement the elephants trumpeted again, threw their trunks down, headed back into line, and marched away—in double-quick time. They were an angry herd as they retreated, pushing over trees, breaking limbs, and rolling rocks down the hillside.

The next morning we continued on into the country toward our destination, the unreached tribe. One day, an ivory hunter came into our camp, and I told him of our experience.

"You did the only known thing that will frighten away elephants," he said. "Beat on a pan or some piece of tin, and they will always run. Shoot at them, and they will always charge."

I hadn't known this that night, but God did, and He dumped all the tin in camp! Some unbelieving or unknowing person might argue that it was merely coincidental. But God desired this experience be used for His glory. We rejoiced over this marvelous deliverance while in Africa. However, God led us, after returning home, to hear the better half of the story:

On one occasion shortly after our arrival in our homeland, I was asked by the lady entertaining us if we had had any unusual experiences while in Africa. We smiled for there were several. She related one experience she had while washing windows at home.

God spoke to her and urgently called her to prayer for us. She hesitated, as one so often does, feeling that her duties were too pressing and her work very important. But God showed her we were in desperate circumstances and in grave danger. She knelt down by the window and poured out her heart to God that He might spare our lives and deliver us from danger. God lifted the burden. It was so unusual an occurrence for her that she wrote down the date and time on her calendar, which she then brought to us.

As we checked it with our own diary, taking into account the nine hours time difference between here and Africa, we were amazed to find that this lady was on her knees interceding for our deliverance while the elephants stood outside our tent. She was 12,000 miles away from us, but close enough to God to be used on our behalf.

PONDER THIS PRINCIPLE: It is important to receive guidance, but there is something even better—TO HAVE A RESIDENT GUIDE. No one can quickly learn all the ways of an African jungle. So, God has promised to be our Helper in times of need.

GOD'S WORD IS OUR COMFORT: How tenderly God soothes our fears. How graciously He says, *Fear thou not; for I am with thee; be not dismayed; for I am thy God...I will uphold thee with the right hand of my righteousness.* He does not say it only once, but He keeps holding our right hand and repeating such promises, *Fear not,...I will help thee* (Isa. 41:10, 13 KJV).

WE PRAY: Father, I am so thankful for those who enter into Your burden of watching over your servants. I thank You for awakening them, and I thank them for being diligent in listening for Your voice.

Focus for Praying

_____
_____
_____
_____
_____
_____
_____
_____
_____
_____
_____
_____
_____
_____
_____
_____
_____

God could intervene without the medium of prayer on the part of another believer, but He has not chosen to do so. We offer these most amazing incidents of miraculous deliverances when God's servants have been traveling abroad on His business. The eye of God is over the righteous. He neither slumbers nor sleeps and is aware of dangers which confront his ambassadors. Surely each has God's protection and His highest interest at heart. Thus He first awakens the intercessor and they obey...

THE IMPULSE TO PRAY

AN INTERCESSOR who compares notes from her diary explains how she was awakened from a deep sleep with an urgent need to pray for two girls traveling in Central Asia. Their mission was to meet and encourage isolated believers, many of whom were without fellowship and the Word of God. This lady had pledged to pray regularly and did so, but this was different, as she later discovered.

Months passed before she found out what had happened on that eventful day. Her two friends traveling in Central Asia were crossing from one country to another. They had entered no-man's land, an uninhabited area, and were driving in the dry, barren desert towards the first police post in the next country.

One of the girls spoke of the apparent lack of traffic on the road. Apart from two soldiers, who were not immediately seen, nobody was at the border entrance. Getting out of the car the two girls went into the small hut to submit their passports for inspection and to request that the road barrier be lifted. Almost instantly the smoky atmosphere was charged with an indescribable, disturbing influence. As the guards talked to each other one of the girls understood the gist of the conversation. Immediately she cried out to God for help, as she gestured for her friend to pray.

It was then they realized it was a holy day and it was most unlikely that anyone from either country would be traveling. The two soldiers continued talking, making their unrepeatable plans for their own indulgences, and then planning the murder of the girls to hide any incriminating evidence. What a predicament!

Though the girls did not entirely understand the language they were very aware of imminent danger. What would God do now? How would He deliver? Was anyone praying for them back home? As the guards examined the passports and made indiscreet comments, suddenly there was noise outside.

In surprise the soldiers looked out of the hut. Their reaction gave new hope to the girls, as they saw an old rusty bus come to a stop at the barrier. It was filled to overflowing with people hanging on to every available bit of metal. As the bus stopped they fell off, their arms, hands and legs tired from hanging on. They swarmed towards the hut. The conversation between the guards was heated.

"Where did they come from? Why were they traveling today?" Angrily they went to investigate. The girls grabbed their passports from the table and dashed out of the hut. In the rush one girl left her handbag behind and raced back to retrieve it. When they reached their car the barrier immediately was lifted and the two girls triumphantly took off.

Why that bus arrived at that moment seemed a mystery. They had no recollection of passing any bus which had to travel slowly. Indeed! The arrival of that bus was timed carefully to coincide with the predicament of the girls. Of course we know the prayers of that elderly sister thousands of miles away had been timed by the greatest Timekeeper of all—Our Lord Jesus—whose perfect timing is so often demonstrated. GOD HAD DONE IT BEFORE. *At midnight Paul and Silas prayed...and immediately all the doors were opened, and every one's bands were loosed.* (Act. 16:25, 26 KJV)

PONDER THIS PRINCIPLE: We know there are those reading this who question the wisdom of two girls getting into such a vulnerable predicament. We answer with R.A Matthews' words, "All opportunities on God's list have a fixed price...SACRIFICE! God does protect those who are on special assignment!" He continues, "A prospective missionary came to the board to ask if it would be possible for them to arrange for him to be sent to an area where the Communists would not come. He wanted to fit his opportunity for service into the limited perspective of personal security, 'If they could arrange for this, he would be in the market; otherwise not at all.'"

HIS PROMISE IS CLEAR: *Go ye therefore, and teach all nations...Teaching them to observe all things...and, lo I am with you alway, even unto the end of the world....* (Matt. 28:19, 20 KJV)

OUR PRAYER: Father, so many people groups in the world still have no Bible nor have they heard the Good News. I do want to live beyond my own neighborhood—beyond my own city and country. Give me a heart like Yours that *"so loved the world."*

ARE YOU WILLING TO STAND IN THE GAP?

Focus for Praying

_____

_____

_____

_____

_____

_____

Most of these incidents have shown how God has worked wonderfully to rescue and restore His servants who were in trouble. Now let me offer my personal testimony of...

GOD'S FAITHFULNESS

ON A Monday afternoon in 1948, a carload of us were leaving a prayer conference in Yakima, Washington. Four of us had enjoyed the fellowship of hundreds who gathered for several days at the fairgrounds.

As we reached the outskirts of the city, a drunken driver speeding in a car he had taken from his employer lost control of the car and hit us head-on. He was instantly killed; a missionary friend riding with us was also killed. Three of us were rushed by ambulance to the hospital in critical condition. Doctors worked feverishly to keep us alive, while area friends who received word of the accident gathered in prayer.

In St. Paul, Minnesota, 2500 miles away, my mother was visiting my sister. They were downtown shopping at this very time when mother suddenly felt strangely moved with inward groanings and travail. She had often felt urges to pray, but this seemed intensely different. Immediately she insisted that they leave their shopping and get home. She felt burdened to cry out to the Lord for someone in her family—she felt someone was in great need.

Two hours passed! Word finally arrived in St. Paul from Yakima. Then Mother discovered that during this perilous time my life was hanging in the balance. The Lord was seeking for her to stand in the gap. Mother gave testimony later that she knew in a new way what Ezekiel meant when he wrote:

> ...*I sought for a man among them, that should make up the hedge, and STAND IN THE GAP before me*.... (Ez 22:30 KJV)

According to this principle of God's working, He searches for someone who will intercede. It is not that a sovereign God must be limited by these laws and principles; He could act according to His own good pleasure. Nonetheless, we discover this most amazing fact in the Bible. He does not move independently, but waits for man to cooperate with Him through prayer.

One of God's servants has explained how God intervenes in these four steps:

– God conceives a thought, which is His will;

– God reveals this will to His children through the Holy Spirit, causing them to know that He has a will, a plan, and an expectation;

– then, God's children return His will by praying to Him, for praying is responding to God's will;

– finally God will accomplish this very thing.

THE PRINCIPLE IS CLEAR: God is the Initiator of all prayer. We are responders to the burden He has given. How often we presume to take the initiative by asking God to fulfill our needs and burdens which He knows better than answering.

GOD'S WORD IS CLEAR: *If any of you lack wisdom, let him ask of God...But let him ask in faith, not wavering. For he that wavereth is like a wave of the sea driven with the wind and tossed. For let not that man think he shall receive any thing of the Lord. A double minded man is unstable in all his ways.* (James 1:5-8 KJV)

WE PRAY: Father, we discover there are many hidden ones who give themselves in intercession. We rejoice! It causes us to ask that we, too, might be available, adjustable and accountable to You for such a ministry...

Throughout these many lessons we have recognized how often God has found responders. We rejoice! There are many hidden ones who will be revealed some day. All of these intercessors have discovered their own weakness, but God's sufficiency. The apostle Paul explains, *Likewise the Spirit also helpeth our infirmities; for we know not what to pray for as we ought: but the Spirit himself maketh intercession for us with groanings which cannot be uttered. And he that searcheth the hearts knoweth what is the mind of the Spirit, because he maketh intercession for the saints according to the will of God.* (Rom. 8:26, 27 KJV)

Focus for Praying

Sometimes because of limited knowledge we must intercede in a general way. When we have an unusual burden for someone we can stand in the gap on their behalf, but we must leave the rest with the One who has called us. In this incident we see God's fingerprints in exact detail. We always rejoice when we meet…

MEN WHO ARE AVAILABLE

A MISSIONARY shared: while serving at a small field hospital in Africa, I traveled every two weeks by bicycle through the jungle to a nearby city for supplies. This required camping overnight halfway. On one of these trips, I saw two men fighting in the city. One was seriously injured, so I treated him and witnessed to him of the Lord Jesus Christ. I then returned home without incident.

Several weeks later upon returning to that city for more supplies, I was approached by the man I had treated earlier. He told me he had known that I carried money and medicine.

He explained, "Some friends and I followed you into the jungle, knowing you would camp overnight. We waited for you to go to sleep and planned to kill you and take your money and drugs. Just as we were about to move into your campsite, we saw that you were surrounded by twenty-six armed guards."

I laughed at this, stating that I was certainly all alone out in the jungle campsite.

The young man pressed the point, "No, sir, I was not the only one to see the guards. My five friends also saw them, and we all counted them. It was because of those guards that we were afraid and left you alone."

At that point of the presentation in a Michigan church, one of the men who was listening jumped up and interrupted the missionary.

"Can you tell me," he asked, "the exact date when this happened?" The missionary thought for a while and recalled the date. The man in the congregation then explained, "On that night in Africa it was morning here. I was preparing to play golf. As I put my bags in the car, I felt the Lord leading me to pray for you. In fact the urging was so strong that I called the men of the church together to pray for you. Will all of those men who met with me that morning please stand?"

The men who had met that morning to pray together stood—there were twenty-six of them!

In these incidents we are convinced that God does intervene to protect those who are on special assignment for Him. But we must honestly face this question—are we available, are we adjustable, are we accountable to God for such participation in His worldwide program?

How do we begin? Each of us should develop our own habit of consistently meeting God. In reading the life-story of many who are dedicated, it seems that morning is the time specially fitted for seeking fellowship with God. It had become the habit for the Psalmist who announces ...*O Lord, in the morning will I direct my prayer unto thee and will look up.* (Psa. 5:3 KJV) Many will testify that giving God the first hour has been best for them.

So, make it your daily habit! When we see the dedication of the Muslim world, we immediately consider why they look down upon the Western world, considering it atheistic. Even in all their blindness, they have the habit of praying regularly many times a day. Of course it has become an empty ritual...but (it seems) they are giving Allah (their god) more attention than many Christians in the West give to Our Father/God.

PONDER THIS PRINCIPLE: To be God-centered is our goal—but it must be Our Father (not Allah) who is the centerpiece of our life. We can prove this by our dedication, our diligence and finally our devotion to Him.

GOD'S WORD IS CLEAR: We have several role models—*Daniel...knelt down on his knees three times that day, and prayed...as was his custom.* (Dan. 6:10 NKJV) It is important to remember: *The effective, fervent prayer of a righteous man avails much.* (James 5:16 NKJV) David said, *As for me, I will call upon God; and the Lord shall save me.*

Evening, and morning and at noon, will I pray, and cry aloud: and He shall hear my voice. (Psa. 55:16, 17 NKJV) They seemed to have developed a habit.

WE PRAY. Father, it is comforting to know that You are the true and living God. We weep for those who call on Allah, but can have no relationship or fellowship with a living Person. Today, we want our dedication to exceed that of the heathen, our diligence to out-measure the world, and our devotion to be demonstrated on our faces and in our walk. Amen!

Focus for Praying

_____

_____

_____

_____

_____

_____

_____

_____

_____

_____

_____

_____

_____

_____

_____

God specializes in rescuing and transforming the most unlikely and makes them trophies of His grace. When we present this story of Chinatown Gertie, it is a demonstration of God's power to very quickly transform a life into amazing fruitfulness. It was so miraculous…

EVERYONE KNEW IT WAS GOD!

IT was during those turbulent years at the turn of the century that a shrewd woman known as Chinatown Gertie kept police on the run. Gertie was a dope addict, a prostitute and, in public opinion, the most vile woman around. Among her own crowd, however, Gertie was something of a queen to her underworld gang who hid out in the dark cellars of Chinatown.

While New Yorkers were reading about Gertie's spine-tingling escapades and wondering what she would do next, an amazing thing happened. Someone from the Chinatown rescue mission got a burden for Gertie. He searched until he found her; then told her the wonderful story of Jesus and His love for her.

Gertie had never heard such a story before. She listened with the eagerness of a child to the words of the gracious invitation, *Come now, and let us reason together…though your sins be as scarlet, they shall be as white as snow; though they be red like crimson, they shall be as wool.* (Isa. 1:18 KJV)

When Gertie learned that Jesus loved her enough to die for her, her heart melted. She made the BIG CHOICE to surrender her life to Him right then. God heard her cry for mercy and instantly broke every chain that bound her, setting her free. Immediately Gertie went to work for her new Master. Such amazing mercy as she had experienced began to flow through her to others. Where once she had been passionate in serving evil she was now as fervent in serving her Lord.

Gertie's years of sin and dissipation had made their mark on her frail body, and the Lord soon called her to Himself. At her funeral in the rescue mission, people filled every seat and lined the walls. From Fifth Avenue, Brooklyn and the Bronx they attended the simple service to gaze upon the face of the woman, now transformed, that they had read so much about. With Gertie's casket open, people marched by in single file to pay respect—line after line—until the building was almost deserted.

As the very last of the viewers departed, an old man approached the casket. He moved closer and when he felt certain that he was alone, he looked into her silent face for a moment. Then, with a deep voice that shattered the silence, he began, "Well, Gertie, I thought I would like to have a little talk with you. Say, Gertie, do you remember that time over in Coney Island when the den was raided? They got me, but you slipped through their hands...." His voice saddened as he reminisced about some of the crimes their gang had pulled off. As he recalled each one he would say, "Do you remember, Gertie?"

Then as he paused for a moment, his faced mellowed. "But then one day somebody told you about Jesus. You repented of your sins and asked Him to forgive you. He washed away all the sin and guilt of your lifetime with His own precious blood. And He put your mind at rest, Gertie.

"You knew you had work to do and not much time to do it. You must have gotten tired going out in the rain and snow and darkness looking for us miserable slaves shackled to the devil. You wanted us to know about the merciful Jesus who could free us, too. You done a good job, Gertie! You did not stop until you had won every last one of our gang to Jesus."

When the old man turned to go, his tear-stained face was radiant. Looking back over his shoulder he said with a loud voice, "So long, Gertie; I'll say goodbye for now. But I'll see you one of these days in heaven—all of us will be there because of you, Gertie! Thanks again—from all of us!"

One day when we stand before the Bema judgment we will all recognize more clearly the POWER OF A RIGHT CHOICE. Now we can recognize the temporal benefits, but then we will appreciate how a surrendered life has magnified the Lord.

PONDER THIS PRINCIPLE: God is seeking to use anyone... anywhere, as much as we allow Him. When we are accountable to Him as Lord of our life, when we are available for difficult tasks, and we are adjustable to His ways and His timing...we can be fruitful!

GOD'S WORD: *For ye see your calling, brethren, how that not many wise men after the flesh, not many mighty, not many noble, are called: But God has chosen the foolish things of the world to confound the wise, and God has chosen the weak things...to confound the things which are mighty.* (1 Cor.1:26, 27 KJV)

WE PRAY: Father from this story I see how important it is that my surrender to You be so complete, there will be no limitation. If you could use Gertie, You can use me. I will!

Why not pray for some friends of your past who need the Lord's transformation in their lives...

Focus for Praying

_____

_____

_____

_____

_____

_____

_____

_____

_____

_____

_____

Looking to the Lord for help is usually much easier than looking to some friend whom He wishes to speak through. So it is mostly a hearing problem—hearing a small child speak for God to urge us to take the...

TIME TO RUN THROUGH THE RAIN

SHE HAD been shopping with her mom in Wal-Mart. She must have been six years old, this beautiful brown-haired, freckle-faced image of innocence. It was pouring rain outside, the kind of rain that gushes over the tops of rain gutters, so much in a hurry to hit the earth that it has no time to flow down the spout. Drains in the nearby parking lot were filled to capacity and some were blocked so that huge puddles laced around parked cars.

We all stood there under the awning, just outside the door of Wal-Mart. We waited—some patiently, others irritated because nature was messing up their hurried day.

Rainfall has always been mesmerizing to me, as I'm absorbed in the sound and sight of the heavens washing away the dirt and dust of the world. Memories of running and splashing as a carefree child came pouring in as a welcome reprieve from the worries of my day.

Her voice was so sweet as it broke the reverie in which we were all caught. "Mom, let's run through the rain," she said.

"What?" Mom asked.

"Let's run through the rain!" she repeated.

"No, honey, we'll wait until it slows down a bit," Mom replied.

This young child waited about another minute and repeated, "Mom, let's run through the rain."

"We'll get soaked if we do," Mom said.

"No, we won't, Mom. That's not what you said this morning," the young girl stated as she tugged at her mom's arm.

"This morning? When did I say we could run through the rain and not get wet?"

"Don't you remember? When you were talking to Daddy about his cancer you said, 'If God can get us through this, He can get us through anything!'"

The entire crowd suddenly hushed in silence as the pounding rain drummed out the only sound. Her mom paused and thought for a moment, considering what she would say. No one came or left in the next few minutes while we all stood quietly.

Now some would laugh it off and scold her for being silly; some might even ignore what had been said. But this was a moment of affirmation in a young child's life, a time when innocent trust could be nurtured so that it would bloom into faith.

The mother finally spoke, "Honey, you are absolutely right. Let's run through the rain. If God lets us get wet, well maybe we just needed washing."

Then off they ran. We all stood watching, smiling and laughing as they darted past the cars and, yes, through the puddles. They held their shopping bags over their heads just in case.

They got soaked.

But they were followed by a few others who screamed and laughed like children all the way to their cars. I want to believe that somewhere down the road in life, Mom will find herself reflecting back on moments they spent together, captured like pictures in the scrapbook of her cherished memories—maybe when she watches proudly as her daughter graduates, or as her daddy walks her down the aisle on her wedding day.

She will laugh again. Her heart will beat a little faster. Her smile will tell the world they love each other. But only they will share that precious moment, when they ran through the rain believing that God would get them through.

And yes, I did. I ran. I got wet. I needed washing.

Take time to run through the rain!

Circumstances or people can take away your material possessions, they can take away your money, and they can even take away your health. But no one can ever take away your precious memories. So don't forget to make time and take the opportunities to make memories every day!

PONDER THIS PRINCIPLE: *Jesus warns, "See that you do not look down on one of these little ones..."* How often through the years I have discovered God was speaking through someone "little in my eyes."

GOD'S WORD IS CLEAR: *Though the Lord is on high, He looks upon the lowly, but the proud He knows from afar.* (Psa. 138:6 NIV)

...Man looks at the outward appearance, but God looks on the heart. (1 Sam. 16:7 NIV). *You are looking on the surface of things...* (2 Cor. 10:7 NIV)

WE PRAY: Father, we are discovering it is not a head problem, but a heart problem. We bow to humble ourselves before You.

Focus on Praying

Some folk seem to have a unique calling for opening hearts. They don't wait for, but make opportunities, to present the gospel. The author has deliberately designed this parable to demonstrate...

THE POWER OF A SINGLE FOCUS

EDITH BURNS was a most amazing lady who lived in San Antonio, Texas. She was the patient of Doctor Will Phillips. Dr. Phillips was a gentle doctor who saw patients as people; he insisted that his favorite patient was Edith Burns.

One morning as he entered his office, he saw her sitting in the waiting room. Edith was there with her big black Bible in her lap earnestly talking to a young mother at her side.

Most marveled at her strange habit of introducing herself, "Hello, my name is Edith Burns; do you believe in Easter?" Then she would explain the meaning of Easter, and many times people would be led to trust Christ.

One day as Dr. Phillips walked into the office he saw the nurse, Beverly, taking Edith's blood pressure. Edith had already introduced herself; then she had asked, "Do you believe in Easter?"

Beverly said, "Why, yes I do."

Edith asked, "Well, what do you believe about Easter?"

Beverly said, "Well, it's about egg hunts, going to church, and dressing up." Edith kept pressing her about the real meaning of Easter, and finally led her to a saving knowledge of Jesus Christ.

When she was called into his office, Edith took one look at the doctor and said, "Dr. Will, why are you so sad? Are you reading your Bible? Are you praying? "

Dr. Phillips said gently, "Edith, I'm the doctor and you're the patient." With a heavy heart he said, "Your lab report came back and it says you have cancer; Edith, you're not going to live long."

Edith exclaimed, "Why Dr. Will, shame on you! Why are you so sad? Do you think God makes mistakes? You have just told me that I am going to soon see my precious Lord Jesus, my husband, and my friends. You have just told me that I am going to celebrate Easter forever, and here you are having difficulty giving me my ticket!"

Dr. Phillips thought to himself. "What a magnificent woman this Edith is!"

Edith continued coming to see Dr. Phillips. The holidays arrived, closing the office for a few days. When it reopened, Edith did not show up; instead, she called Dr. Phillips and said she would have to be moving her story to the hospital and then explained, "Doctor, I'm very near home, so would you make sure that they put women next to me in my room that need to hear about Easter?"

Well, they did just that! Would you believe it? Every woman who shared that room with Edith came to trust Christ. Everyone on that floor from staff to patients became so excited about Edith that they started calling her Edith Easter; that is, everyone except Phyllis Cross, the head nurse.

Phyllis made it plain that she wanted nothing to do with Edith, because she was a "religious nut." She had served as a nurse in an army hospital; she was the original G.I. Jane who had been married three times. She had seen and heard it all. Phyllis was hard and cold, and did everything by the book.

One morning the two nurses scheduled to attend Edith were sick. Edith needed attention and Phyllis Cross had to go in and give her a shot. When she walked in, Edith had a big smile on her face and said, "Phyllis, God loves you and I love you, and I have been praying for you."

Phyllis Cross responded, "Well, you can quit praying for me, it won't work. I am not interested."

Edith said, "Well, I will pray and I have asked God not to let me go home until you come into the family."

Phyllis said, "Then you will never die, because that will never happen." And she curtly walked out of the room.

One day Phyllis said she was literally drawn to Edith's room like a magnet drawn to iron. She sat down on the bed and Edith said, "I'm so glad you have come, because God told me that today is your special day."

Phyllis Cross said, "Edith, you have asked everybody here the question, 'Do you believe in Easter?' But you have never asked me."

Edith replied, "Phyllis, I wanted to many times, but God told me to wait until you asked—and now you have asked."

Edith took her Bible and explained the Easter story of Jesus Christ's death and resurrection. Edith asked, "Phyllis, do you believe in Easter? Do you believe that Jesus Christ is alive and He wants to live in your heart?"

Phyllis answered, "Yes, I do!" Right then, Phyllis prayed and invited Jesus into her heart. For the first time Phyllis did not walk out of a hospital room; she was carried out on the wings of angels.

When Phyllis arrived two days later, Edith asked, "Do you know what day it is?"

Phyllis answered, "Why Edith, its Good Friday."

Edith interrupted, "Oh no, for you—every day is Easter. Happy Easter, Phyllis!"

Two days later, on Easter Sunday, Phyllis headed to the florist after work to get some Easter lilies for Edith. When she walked into Edith's room, she lay quietly in bed with the big black Bible on her lap. Her hands were in the Bible—a sweet smile was on her face. As Phyllis picked up her hand, she realized Edith was dead.

Her left hand was on John 14:2, 3, *In my Father's house are many mansions...I go to prepare a place for you...I will come again, and receive you to myself, that where I am, there ye may be also.* (KJV)

Her right hand was on Revelation 21:4, *And God shall wipe away all tears from their eyes, and there shall be no more death neither sorrow, nor crying neither shall there be any more pain; for the former things are passed away.* (KJV)

Phyllis Cross looked at that dead body, and then lifted her face toward heaven, and with tears streaming down her cheeks, said, "Happy Easter, Edith, Happy Easter!"

Phyllis walked out of the room, and over to a table where two student nurses were sitting. She said, "My name is Phyllis Cross. Do you believe in Easter?"

PONDER THIS PRINCIPLE: There's something so very contagious about a life poured out to please the Lord, about lips that are dedicated to magnify Him. Life begets life. Notice how Phyllis was first awakened, then captured and finally she was "single-ized." (That is my special word for one who has a single eye that is focused.)

GOD'S WORD: *For where your treasure is, there will your heart be also. ...if therefore thine eye be single, thy whole body shall be full of light...No man can serve two masters....* (Matt. 6:21, 22, 24 KJV)

WE PRAY: Father, my goal is to be so captured by You that I will develop a single eye—yes, be "single-ized" in my purpose. Amen!

Focus for Praying

_____
_____
_____
_____
_____
_____
_____
_____
_____
_____
_____
_____
_____
_____
_____
_____
_____
_____
_____
_____
_____
_____

When God is looking down on each day of your life, do you think He is still questioning whether you understand His purposes for you? Is His heart grieved because so few really understand and are seeking Him? (Psa. 14:2, 3) In this lesson we see how sovereignly God works through a young man who is committed to making Him known. We can recognize that God is working, by one of the fingerprints He leaves—He does everything...

RIGHT ON TIME

ROGER SIMMS had just left the military and was eager to take his uniform off once and for all. Now he was hitchhiking home, and his heavy duffel bag made the trip even more arduous than the normal hitch. Flashing his thumb to an oncoming car, he lost hope when he saw that it was a shiny, black, expensive car, so new that it had a temporary license in the back window. It was hardly the type of car that would stop for a hitchhiker.

But to his amazement, the car stopped and the passenger door opened. He ran toward the car, placed his duffel carefully in the back, and slid into the leather front seat. He was greeted by the friendly smile of a handsome older gentleman with distinguished gray hair and a deep tan.

"Hello, son. Are you on leave or are you going home for good?"

"I just got out of the army, and I'm going home for the first time in several years," answered Roger.

"Well, you're in luck if you're going to Chicago," smiled the man.

"Not quite that far," said Roger, "but my home is on the way. Do you live there, Mister?"

"My name is Hanover; yes, I have a business there." And with that, they were on their way.

After sharing brief life histories and talking about everything under the sun, Roger (who was a Christian) felt a strong compulsion to witness to Mr. Hanover about Christ. But witnessing to an elderly, wealthy businessman who obviously had everything he could ever want was a scary prospect indeed. Roger kept putting it off, but nearing his destination forced the issue.

"Mr. Hanover," began Roger, "I would like to tell you something very important." He then proceeded to explain the way of salvation, ultimately asking Mr. Hanover if he would like to receive Christ as his Savior. To Roger's astonishment, the big car pulled over to the side of the road; Roger thought for a moment that Mr. Hanover was about to throw him out. Then a strange and wonderful thing happened—the businessman bowed his head and began to cry, affirming that he did in fact want to receive Christ into his heart. As he later dropped Roger at his house, he thanked him explaining, "This is the greatest thing that has ever happened to me."

Five years went by and Roger Simms found himself packing for a business trip to Chicago. In the process, he came across a small gold-embossed business card which Mr. Hanover had given him years earlier. When Roger arrived in Chicago, he looked up Hanover Enterprises, and found it to be located downtown in a tall, prominent building. The receptionist told him that it would be impossible to see Mr. Hanover, but that if he was an old friend, he would be able to see Mrs. Hanover. A little disappointed, he was led into a poshly decorated office where a woman in her fifties was sitting at a huge oak desk.

She extended her hand. "You knew my husband?" Then Roger explained how Mr. Hanover had been kind enough to give him a ride back home.

A look of interest passed across her face. "Can you tell me what date that was?"

"Sure," said Roger. "It was May 7th, five years ago, the day I was discharged from the army."

"And did anything special happen on your ride...anything unusual?"

Roger wondered if there had been some source of contention between the two, which resulted in a marital breakup or separation. But once again, he felt the prompting of the Lord to be truthful. "Mrs. Hanover, your husband received the Lord into his heart that day. I explained the gospel message to him and he pulled to the side of the road and wept, then chose to pray a prayer of salvation."

Suddenly, she burst into tears, sobbing uncontrollably. After several minutes, she regained control to explain, "I grew up in a Christian home, but my husband did not. I had prayed for his salvation for many years, and I believed God would save him. But just after he let you out of his car on May 7th, he passed away in a horrible head-on collision. He never arrived home. I thought God had not kept His promise, and I stopped living for the Lord five years ago because I blamed Him for not keeping His word."

Someone reading this—even now—may have allowed disappointment into your heart because God (seemingly) did not fulfill your expectations. Promises are the foundation of our hope. A child's security depends on a parent's promise to keep him safe. A spouse can live with confidence because of a mate's promise of fidelity, loyalty and love. Businesses depend on promises from employees, vendors, and clients. It is most unfortunate when they are not kept; hearts are broken, and bitterness develops. There is one Promise Maker, though, who can be trusted completely and without fear. Our Father/God has given us hundreds of promises in His Word, and He keeps every one of them.

PONDER THIS PRINCIPLE: It is not God's plan that we just thumb through His word and claim random verses as personal promises. There is a difference between our grasping a verse, (a logos-word) and God's giving us a promise (rhema—a quickened word). I know this may be difficult for some of you to accept, but through long years of experience I know the importance. Are you looking for hope? Then search the Scriptures diligently. When God quickens a verse that applies to you, claim it as a foundation upon which you can stand. When you have received His quickened word—you know that you know that you know.

GOD'S WORD IS CLEAR: *Consider how Abraham ...did not waver at the promise of God through unbelief.* (Rom. 4:20 NIV) There is no other way to explain his steadfast confidence. Through many years and many contrary circumstances he maintained his position—God would give him a son! It was more than a verse; it had been a quickened promise. No wonder we call him FATHER OF THE FAITH!

WE PRAY: Father we know Your desire for a family of sons who are conformed to the likeness of our Lord Jesus. We desire this same commitment that we see in Roger Simms.

Focus for Praying

One day we will face a rude awakening. We discover that our love for people will not sustain diligence or faithfulness. We simply run out of love (human-phileo), because people are difficult and unappreciative. The Apostle Paul understood this when He wrote, "*...the love of Christ compels us...*" To demonstrate this, Pastor Ben Hayden shares two testimonies resulting in ...

AMAZING FAITHFULNESS

IT HAPPENED like this! One night the rescue mission director in London invited testimonies from the audience. A serviceman stood up and shared how his ship was docked in Sydney, Australia. While on leave, he was walking the streets one night when an old man approached him and asked, "If you were to die tonight, do you know where you would spend eternity?" That was all he said, just one very pointed question—and then the old man melted into the crowd.

Several months later another serviceman came into this same rescue mission giving a similar testimony. He explained how an old man in Sydney, Australia had approached him on the street and asked this same question and then vanished into the crowd. In both instances these men told how that feeble but pointed witness started them thinking about eternity and spiritual matters. Each eventually trusted Christ and was diligent in sharing his witness.

Some time later, this rescue mission director was in Sydney for an international convention of mission directors. He remembered the two testimonies of these servicemen and determined he would try to find that old man who had witnessed on the streets. He was eager to explain to him about these two conversions.

Night after night the mission director walked the streets of Sydney looking, and was on the verge of giving up hope that the old man could be found. Then by divine appointment it happened. That final night just before departing for London, this old man approached him and politely asked, "If you were to die tonight, where would you spend eternity?"

At last...at last he had found him! He rejoiced that now he could tell him what an important part he had played in the conversion of the two servicemen.

That elderly gentleman was amazed! With tearful eyes he responded, "I have given my witness with stammering tongue for over fifty years. This is the first time I have heard that anyone has been affected by my ministry."

Did this elderly man have a prophetic voice that penetrated the heart? It would seem he did. We are sure of this. It was not the appreciation from people, but it was his undying love for the Lord that compelled him for fifty years. One day in eternity he will discover his eternal reward, yet it seemed our Father/God wanted to reward him now with encouragement, so he burdened that mission director to diligently seek and find him.

PONDER THIS PRINCIPLE: Perhaps you are now facing a down moment and have been questioning the effectiveness of your own labors. Pause! Hear His gentle voice speaking, "Just follow Me...I know your heart. I know your burden...look away from your seeming failure and disappointments. Keep occupied with Me...that is what matters most. Remember! I am even more concerned about winning lost souls than you are. I have much more invested than you have. Keep faithful...and you will one day hear, "Well done, thou faithful servant; enter into thy reward."

GOD'S WORD: There have been many through the centuries, though unknown to us now, who will discover their reward. Do you recall the words of Boaz when he spoke to Ruth about her faithfulness? *The Lord recompense thy work, and a full reward be given thee of the Lord God of Israel, under whose wings thou are come to trust.* (Ruth 2:12 KJV)

WE PRAY: Father, all that I have come to know of You gives me perfect confidence to wholly trust You. Amen!

Focus for Praying

Father must be delighted when He sees how some of His kids have learned to handle their limitations. We can all take heart that God is available to supply every need. But we must recognize the secret for receiving. Now, I want to introduce Lola Lamereau and let her tell you about three unusual friends she calls...

MY THREE GRACES

MY FIRST grace is Helen; she is a polio victim. For twenty years she has propelled herself about with hand crutches or a wheelchair. She manages her home, cooks, sews for her two daughters and herself, and drives a manual car. I have never seen Helen discontented or out of sorts. She smiles—in fact her face beams, and just to look at her, you know she is a happy person.

Not long ago we were having coffee together in her home. She went to the kitchen for something and slid on the linoleum, falling flat. "I'll have to do this myself," she said as I rushed out to help her. After resting a bit she sat up and, with her hands, scooted herself through the dining room, the living room, and out to the hall where she seated herself on the lowest stair tread and thus raised herself up. She was out of breath. What she had done hadn't been easy.

For the first time I mentioned her disability. With tears in my eyes I said, "Oh Helen, it's awful to be so handicapped, isn't it?"

"You mustn't say that, Lola," she answered firmly. Then she smiled at me. "When I look about me and see so many people worse off than I am, I'm thankful for all the things I can do."

What a lesson Helen taught me! The apostle Paul expresses it... *for I have learned in whatever state I am...to be content.* (Phil. 4:11 NKJV)

So we recognize her secret! In turning from her limitations and problems, Helen has occupied herself with Him. The Greek word "aphorao" explains this; it means "turning from to continually behold." Until now we may not have realized how many of our friends have demonstrated this grace.

THEN there is Greta, my beloved blind friend. She is sixty years old and has been totally without sight for forty of those years. I can't pity her; I can only admire her and treasure her friendship. She talks freely of her blindness, but usually ends by saying, "Don't feel sorry for me, I have it made. Think of all the taped and recorded books and magazines I have to read. I hear the news and the ads on the radio and the telephone keeps me in touch with my friends."

Greta earned her college degree about ten years ago. Now she teaches a class in European history in a small college. Because of her fine attitude she has many friends who help her by reading to her on tape from the textbooks.

One day when I was leaving her home she walked out on the porch with me. It was spring and had rained the night before. Greta took a deep breath. "Doesn't spring smell wonderful?" she asked. "And listen to the birds. Wouldn't it be terrible to be deaf? Just think of not being able to hear the joyous sounds of nature, not to be able to carry on a conversation with people or to hear good music. I'm blessed; truly I am."

"Greta," I thought to myself, "I am so fortunate to have you as a friend. You do fulfill Paul's exhortation, *Rejoice in the Lord alway, and again I say Rejoice. And the peace of God, which passeth all understanding, shall keep your hearts and minds through Christ Jesus.*" (Phil. 4:4, 7 KJV)

What a demonstration of "aphorao"—refusing to be occupied with her own difficult circumstances. She was occupied with Him! What a way to enjoy God's supply of grace.

And then there is Lucretia. She has no handicaps. She has an unusually fine mind, a strong body, and plenty of material wealth. She can lead almost any kind of a life she chooses. And what does she choose? She makes opportunities to be outgoing and outgiving. She reads many hours a week for Greta on tapes. She drives out of her way to pick up Jack and take him to the Writer's Club; he has no way of getting there on his own. Or if something unpleasant must be done, Lucretia simply states, "I'll do it; I have time."

Recently I told her, "Lucretia, you are so generous in every way; surely there are times when you'd rather do something for yourself."

Lucretia simply smiles. "Everyone has an equal number of hours to spend. Maybe I'm selfish; I use my time the way that makes me the happiest."

Selfish? No, she's found a way of tapping into the joy of living. It comes when one turns from self-centered living and becomes occupied with the needs of others. When you discover this secret you recognize that in seeking happiness as your goal you will miss it. It is the by-product of living unto God and serving others.

Helen, Greta, Lucretia—they are three lovely graces. Everyone who observes them will agree they are trophies of His grace.

PONDER THIS: One day we shall be amazed! All these little people, unseen people, largely unknown to others—God is using them to be a channel of blessing. Some day when God reveals all the hidden things, we shall be amazed at His vast company of redeemed servants.

GOD'S WORD: The apostle Paul gives this summary of His service:

...it is required that those who have been given a trust must prove faithful. I care very little if I am judged by you or by

any human court; indeed I do not even judge myself...It is the Lord who judges me... (1 Cor. 4:2 NIV)

WE PRAY: Father, it is not so important that men see our labors and commend us. Help each of us to live under Your watchful eye... seeking only to please You.

Focus for Praying

_____
_____
_____
_____
_____
_____
_____
_____
_____
_____
_____
_____
_____
_____
_____
_____
_____
_____
_____
_____

In this lesson we come to the ultimate relationship: We know why the heavenly Father finds such delight in His Son, the Lord Jesus. But here we see why an earthly father finds such enjoyment in his son. David Morken shares this intimate moment of how his son…

MADE A WISE CHOICE

WHEN our eldest son, Hubert, was a little fellow, we were visiting Balboa in southern California. One day we went to see the beautiful ships in the harbor; Hubert seemed to want every one of them.

He would say with boyish excitement, "Oh, Daddy, wouldn't you like to have that one? And he would point his chubby finger at a gleaming motor cruiser—or sleek sailboat. As we approached a bigger, more luxurious vessel that probably cost over a million, again Hubert said, "Daddy, wouldn't you like to have that one?"

"Hubert," I replied, "let me ask you a question. Suppose a man were to come to Daddy and say, 'Mr. Morken, I want to give you a choice between two things. You may become owner of all these ships in the harbor, and we'll add to them the *Queen Mary,* the *Queen Elizabeth,* and all the ships of the President lines. (Hubert was interested in ocean liners!) Furthermore, I will give you enough money to operate them all. That's the first choice. Or, (and I pointed to Hubert) you may have this little boy.' Now which do you think Daddy would choose?"

Without a moment's hesitancy my son replied, "Why, Daddy, I think you'd choose me." He looked at me with his big brown eyes and added, "Because you love me."

I said, "Hubert, this is part of the reason."

"What's the other part?" he asked.

"The other part is that you love me. If you owned that beautiful ship, we might have a lot of fun aboard it, but we could never love it, because wood and brass cannot receive love nor give love. The ship could never love us; it has no ability to love anything."

I asked Hubert, "Do you know why you are worth more to God than all the stars in the heavens?"

"No," he replied.

"Because," I explained, "God made the stars, and the biggest and brightest among them can be enjoyed by us all. They can be studied and measured by the scientists. God knows their names, but they cannot receive love, nor can they love God—or anyone else. But you can!"

It is now almost sixty years ago that I invited David Morken to be our Saturday night YFC speaker in Salem, Oregon. There was a spiritual quality in him that was immediately evident. As I recall he encouraged me to invite one of his best friends,

Hubert Mitchell to be one of our speakers. I did and we enjoyed him just as much. I offer this because David named this son from our story after his friend, Hubert.

In this loving response of a father and son we recognize the unique relationship God has planned with His family. God gives to us all that really matters—Himself; we in return give to Him—ourselves. All the things in this universe rightfully take second place, and PERSONS take center-stage—the Father and His Family!

Consider this—if mere things could have satisfied King Solomon, his kingly position with its glory and fame, his vast wealth and his amazing wisdom would have been enough. But he pronounced it all vanity of vanities. Likewise, if mere things could have satisfied the heart of God, the whole vast universe was before Him. But God desired more; because of His very personhood, He desired fellowship. By divine intention and design every personality is so constituted that it requires the mutual response of fellowship. So there is a need for pure love and mingling of our spirit with His Spirit that reaches out as an enormous vacuum to be filled.

PONDER THIS PRINCIPLE: Let us restate it again. An indescribable "deep" within every breast reaches out as an enormous vacuum to be filled; but there is also a "Deep" within God which is calling out for fulfillment and satisfaction. We were made for God and only God can fit into the "great empty space within man."

GOD'S WORD IS CLEAR: When the psalmist wrote, *Deep calls unto deep at the call of the fountainhead...* (Fenton) we have David's attempt to describe this spiritual "longing." Something (deep) within God and deep within man—each is calling out for the other. But it is interesting that God is THE Fountainhead; He is the first one to call. And man has been responding in many ways ever since.

Consider one more attempt to explain this mystery. Eccl. 3:11 states, *He has made everything beautiful in its time; also He has set eternity in their hearts...* (NKJV). Who can explain this "eternity" in our hearts? Every man has it—and will forever try to give it meaning.

WE PRAY: Father, once again we are shut up to You for a greater measure of revelation. We join Paul in exulting, *O the depth of the riches both of the wisdom and knowledge of God! how unsearchable are his judgments, and his ways past finding out!* (Rom. 11:33 KJV)

Focus for Praying

God is looking? He is looking upon His entire family to see if there are character qualities in us—to see if there are virtues which bear the likeness of His Son. In this lesson we discover one who truly seemed to...

MAINTAIN HIS FOCUS

ONE evening a couple of years ago, I was about to turn off the TV as the evening news finished. But in that brief moment I saw the Billy Graham crusade flash onto the screen. It was an evening service from Dallas, now several months later being replayed.

We listened to several musical renditions and then heard the familiar voice of Franklin Graham as he announced, "Tonight we have a special treat for you. My father's brother, Melvin, will share a testimony before my dad speaks." My attention was immediately glued to the screen as I remembered Melvin from forty-nine years earlier when I was in Charlotte, North Carolina.

I recalled the circumstances that lead to our meeting. Each night I was speaking in a church, and it had been my joy to teach a Bible lesson each morning to a large gathering of ladies in Mrs. Givens' home. One morning at the close of our lesson, Mrs. Graham (Billy's mother) came and asked, "If I bring my son, Melvin, to the class tomorrow would you have some time to spend with him?" I assured her I would be delighted.

The next morning when I met Melvin I explained that I had known his mother and father for several years. It had also been my privilege years earlier to invite Billy and his team to a large outdoor Youth for Christ rally at a ballpark in Salem, Oregon, prior to Billy's sudden escalation into national prominence. Now it was my present joy to meet Melvin.

As I looked into his sober face, he began to share, "Many years ago when Billy was sixteen and I was eleven, we attended a meeting conducted by Mordecai Hamm. We were both saved. Since then you know how Billy was thrust into the evangelical spotlight these years with a ministry that reaches many thousands. But I have been isolated at home with my parents, milking cows, tending a dairy farm—and wondering what God has for my life."

I could imagine many deep concerns in his heart. I knew his mother and father were not only dedicated to the welfare of their family, but claiming God's best for each son and daughter. Since the moment I'd been asked to meet him, I had been seeking the Lord for some encouraging word to share with Melvin.

I began, "You know Melvin, there is only one thing we need to consider." As I recall, I opened my Bible to read this statement I had copied years earlier, "On his deathbed, one of the spiritual giants who has caught the attention of the religious world whispered, 'Perhaps the greatest thing I have learned in my lifetime is my personal ACCOUNTABILITY TO GOD.' Melvin, the apostle Paul also made this very clear to me when he wrote, '...*it is required in stewards, that a man be found faithful.*' Melvin, you have your gifting and calling from God, and I have mine."

God is very sovereign in His choosing; this is something that remains a mystery to me—to all of us. I am sure many who know of Billy's effective ministry wonder about Melvin—what is he doing for God? I think as I look back through the years that many of us ponder (almost jealously) how Billy got chosen for the spotlight—while most of us remain largely unknown.

I can still see in my mind's eye that pensive look on Melvin's face. Was I touching a tender place? It was tender to me—and I felt sure he faced the same question. "Melvin, when you and I stand before the BEMA judgment to be evaluated for our service, only one thing will count. Have I been faithful; have you been FAITHFUL IN YOUR CALLING? Melvin, you must not try to fulfill the expectations of others. You have your own gifting and calling... carefully heed that and BE FAITHFUL. Paul continues to write, '...*it is a very small thing that I should be judged of you or of man's judgment: yea I judge not mine own self.*'" (1 Cor. 4:2, 3 KJV)

94

There were other things we talked about, and this conversation is so long ago I trust I have been correct in my recall. But I felt assured when Melvin left—his heart was lighter and his countenance brighter.

The next morning before the Bible study started, Mrs. Graham came to me asking this question, "What did you say to Melvin yesterday? All day long his countenance was different; he was joyful and cheerful—he seemed contented." Then she added, "You know I have a daughter, I would like to bring her tomorrow..." And she did!

I have been hesitant in sharing this story, for I have not wanted to appear as a name-dropper—nor do I want to imply that I was any great counselor. But the amazing timing in seeing that Billy Graham crusade from Dallas and hearing Melvin as he shared his testimony still brings joy and encouragement to my heart.

Melvin began, "You know Billy and I attended a revival crusade...Billy was 16 and I was 11 when we were saved. You all realize how God has used my brother and he is known throughout the world...but I have been at home, following my own gifting and calling. I have pondered this many times. God alone knows what I may have done for Him—but I have above all sought to be FAITHFUL. I am accountable to Him."

AMAZING! I recognized those very same words I had given to him that morning as we had visited so many years ago. Then I looked up my message journal where I had recorded these dates—March 17-24, 1957—and the titles of the messages given those mornings at Mrs. Givens' and in the evenings at the C and M Alliance church.

It was only a few weeks later I discovered that Melvin went home to meet His Lord shortly after that Dallas appearance. I was most grateful, for it seemed to me that he had kept his focus on things eternal.

PONDER THIS PRINCIPLE: Some day when we stand before our Lord to give an account, as God's fellow workers we will discover how much of our labor has passed the test of fire. Everything that is wood, hay and stubble will burn; but everything that is gold, silver and precious stones will abide. Don't compare yourself with anyone else, for God will reward each one according to his faithfulness in his own calling.

GOD'S WORD: Paul writes, *People should think of us as servants of Christ, the ones God has trusted with His secrets. Now in this way those who are trusted with something valuable must show they are worthy of that trust. As for myself, I do not care if I am judged by you or any human court...The Lord is the one who judges me. So do not judge before the right time; wait until the Lord comes. He will bring to light things that are now hidden in darkness, and will make known the secret purposes of people's hearts. Then God will praise each one of them.* (1 Cor. 4:1-5 NCV)

WE PRAY: Father, we know You are looking down upon all of us—hoping to see the likeness of Your Son formed in us. Today I choose to SHARPEN MY FOCUS on what will bring most delight to You.

Focus for Praying

_____
_____
_____
_____
_____
_____
_____
_____
_____
_____
_____
_____
_____
_____
_____
_____
_____
_____

God is ever looking for the character qualities of His Son in our lives. Sometimes we are growing, but often lopsidedly, with certain virtues out of proportion. All wise men have recognized this asymmetry and have sought to correct it, by preaching one form or another of the "golden mean" doctrine. A French philosopher explained, "No man is strong unless he bears within his character antithesis strongly marked." So, each virtue must be balanced by its opposite virtue and held in living tension. Our spiritual growth depends on how we deal with these tensions in developing ...

BALANCED VIRTUES

THOUGH we had often been together as speakers on a platform, it was our first time to enjoy table fellowship with our wives. During the conversation my friend lovingly exhorted his wife, "Dearie, just give the headlines and save the details for later." We all smiled and I realized he was a man who could hold the larger perspective and keep details in their proper place. Just a bit later I observed another balance God had wrought. I saw him demonstrate the ability to show compassion while exerting necessary firmness (I like to call it tough-love.) Finally during our intense discussion I sensed his careful discernment (an intuitive quality we all need), even as he was carefully weighing principles in a most rational way.

Quickly I want to summarize these balancing virtues which were evident in this colleague: compassion with firmness, perspective yet with details, and a wonderful mystical awe to balance his rational approach. These balanced virtues are the mark of spiritual maturity we will consider in this lesson.

Every Christian is a saint in embryo. The heavenly genes are in him and the Holy Spirit is working to bring him into a spiritual balance that accords with the nature of the Heavenly Father from whom he received the deposit of divine life. We must recognize that in this mortal body—subject to weakness and temptation—God invites our cooperation in making us balanced. So both our will and our intelligence must be continually involved. We must recognize that God's remedy for our imbalance is not a new philosophy but a NEW LIFE.

This means that we are daily transformed by the renewing of our minds and being conformed to the likeness of Christ. We can be grateful—very grateful—that the center of our faith and our loyalty is the most balanced Character ever seen on our planet. As we keep our focus on Jesus we will see these antithesis strongly marked.

* Jesus was both militant and passive—militant in that He was projecting the most redemptive movement, the Kingdom of God, into the total life to effect a total change; passive in that He unresistingly went to a cross without a murmur or complaint.

*He was both world-renouncing and world-participating—world-renouncing in that He could say, "I am not of this world"; world-participating in that He lived His life out in intimate human relationships and finally died for the world.

* He was tender and He was terrible—tender in that He wept over a city and at the grave of His friend; terrible in that He drove the usurpers out of His Father's house with whipcords of tongue and lash.

*He was a man of prayer and man of action—of prayer in that He spent whole nights in prayer; of action in that "He went about doing good."

*He was both self-renouncing and self-asserting—self-renouncing in that He "emptied Himself" and self-asserting in that He said, "I am the way, the truth, and the life." In our Lord Jesus we see both the Lamb and the Lion. As the Lamb He is meek and mild; as the Lion He is kingly and aggressive.

It has been stated so often—we become like that which we worship. As an example, consider those who keep looking at Allah, the false god of the Muslim world. You wonder about their fierce devotion to sovereignty, and the demand for total (blind) submission to Allah, which eventuates in fatalism (what will be will be).

Now consider the secular Western world which has developed a caricature of the true God. For the most part western man is now bowing at the shrine of his RIGHT TO TOTAL FREEDOM. Sadly, this becomes a raw humanism that proudly boasts "we can do it" without God. Freedom is indeed the blessing of democracies, but western man has become so occupied with his total freedom FROM, that he has largely ignored what this freedom is FOR. Only the dedicated Christian knows that he is responsible to God and His kingdom.

THE FINAL CONFLICT of the ages is now upon us. Only as we uncover the deception of both the Islamic world and the Western world can we discover God's way. How shall we answer these extremes of total submission and total freedom? We see in our God that He is above all THE FATHER who wisely purposes PATERNAL SOVEREIGNTY but also PATERNAL MORALITY (freedom). There is something so attractive about BALANCED VIRTUES, which means the genes of our Father/God are displayed in a believer's life. We must boldly insist upon this spiritual approach. Only a spiritual militancy will conquer where nothing else can.

I have never forgotten a visit with Dr A.W. Tozer when his balanced virtues became so evident. He explains how often in our effort to be right, we may go wrong—so wrong as to lead to spiritual deformity...

1...when in our determination to be bold we
become brazen. Yes, courage and meekness are

compatible qualities; both were found in perfect proportion in Christ. Peter before the Sanhedrin and Paul before Agrippa demonstrated both qualities, though on another occasion when Paul's boldness temporarily lost its charity and became carnal he said to the high priest, Ananias, *"God shall smite thee, thou whited wall."* It is to the credit of the apostle Paul that when he saw what he had done he immediately apologized (Acts 23:1-5 KJV)

2...when in our desire to be frank we become rude. Candor without rudeness was always found in the Lord Jesus. The Christian who boasts that he always calls a spade a spade is likely to end by calling everything a spade. Even the fiery Peter learned that love does not blurt out everything it knows. (1 Pet. 4:8)

3...when in our effort to be watchful we become suspicious. Because there are many adversaries, the temptation is to see enemies where none exist. Because we are in conflict with error we tend to develop a spirit of hostility to everyone who disagrees with us on anything.

4...when we seek to be serious we become somber. The saints have always been serious, but gloominess is a defect of character and should not be equated with godliness. Religious melancholy may indicate the presence of unbelief or sin and if long continued may lead to mental disturbance. Joy is a great therapeutic for the mind. *Rejoice in the Lord always....* (Phil. 4:4 KJV)

5...when we mean to be conscientious we become over-scrupulous. If the devil cannot succeed in destroying the conscience he will settle for making it sick. We have observed Christians who are so fearful they may displease God, they live in constant distress. (AWT)

Finally, we must recognize this: spiritual balance is not our goal. Having balanced virtues within ourselves is God's work which can only be accomplished as we learn to hear His voice.

PONDER THIS PRINCIPLE: We look at our Lord Jesus, who is God's window to show us the Father. In Him we see balanced virtues that are so attractive. Be careful; it is not in being preoccupied with ourselves but in making Him the constant focus of our lives that God will structure our daily obedience to form the balanced virtues of Christ in us.

GOD'S WORD: Hebrews 12:2 shows us how by...*Looking unto Jesus the author and the finisher...* (KJV)—the One who starts and completes all things. There are three Greek words for looking:

> "blepo" means "a passing glance",
>
> "horao" means "a steady gaze" and
>
> "aphorao" means a "turning from to continually behold."

In Hebrews 12:15 we read—*Looking diligently, lest any man fail of the grace of God...* (KJV) Here the word is "aphorao", which means we are "turning from" to be wholly occupied with HIM.

WE PRAY: Father, we have one concern. That You might see the likeness of Your Son in us. We acknowledge YOUR GIFT to us—that Jesus indwells each of us. Now we offer OUR GIFT to You—what we have become.

Focus for Praying

_____

_____

_____

_____

_____

_____

_____

_____

_____

I AM A DEBTOR...

AS I look back over my journey I am so thankful to God for many teachers who have influenced my life. Some touched me in a casual way, some deeply impressed me, but others had an eternal impact upon me. It is so true that we are a part of all we have ever met.

During my teenage years C.A. Jones (who later became my father-in-law) crowded me continually to recognize and live in the "Larger Purpose Box." In his life and ministry I saw a dedication to cooperate with our Father/God that He might receive many sons—all conformed to the image of His Pattern-Son.

At a most critical juncture in my life, I became involved with T.S. Sparks of London. His fatherly counsel for many years, both here and in Europe, exposed my tendency to "push things to extremes." I observed his balance as we often prayed before entering a meeting, "Lord, we need an open heaven. Do help us to live in the good of all that we know."

When I spent a couple of months at Cannon Beach, Oregon, directing students from Prairie Bible Institute in beach evangelism, I heard them repeat their president, L. E. Maxwell's, constant reminder. They affectionately called it Maxwell 1:1 "Keep balanced." Then I met him, and I recognized he was a man of very strong convictions. Did he live up to his motto on balance? I feel sure that our God would answer; "Yes, he is one in whom I take much delight."

For years I was impacted by the writings of A. W. Tozer. Then I met this prophet whose voice had so painfully exposed the carnal methods of the evangelical world. I had assumed him to be like a modern John the Baptist, yet I found him to be soft, gentle and easily entreated. He had previously criticized my early book, THE ULTIMATE INTENTION as being too idealistic. But this misunderstanding was rectified and I continue to this day to thank God for his balance. Tozer was a modern mystic, yet he was so practical and wholly rational.

There are a dozen more whom I should acknowledge for their distinctive impact in my life; many are still alive today. Yet I especially want to thank God for the writings of a man I never met. Watchman Nee and his many books represent a most unusual balance. As I have moved through many countries, I am constantly amazed at the deep spiritual impact of his life not only among the Chinese but also many others in the Body of Christ.

FINALLY, I must say with Paul—I am a debtor! No words could ever express my appreciation for those who have patiently helped me through the years. All of us have this one thing in common: we are determined that OUR HEAVENLY FATHER SHALL SEE IN US THE CHARACTER VIRTUES OF HIS SON.

WE ARE PARTNERS IN SHARING…

A doctor in the Atlanta area went to his pastor when he had finished the "fifteen day prayer journey." He asked for more copies, since the pastor had recently ordered several cartons.

The doctor had so enjoyed the challenge to pray for others that he determined to send a book to his sister for whom he had been diligently interceding. In his haste to get a book packaged for her, he doubled his prayer time in asking the Lord to awaken his sister to see her spiritual need to trust Christ. He hoped the stories would capture her attention even as they had stirred him.

About ten days later he received a phone call from his sister, the object of his prayers. There had never been much serious fellowship in previous years because she felt he was too religious, but that day on the phone…things were different. Her initial greeting was warm, and she finally blurted out, "I did not know you were so concerned for me to pray for me every day. I see by your own admission how you have been asking God to "save my soul." Well, I must tell you that at first I was really offended. You know I have felt you were becoming a religious kook, instead of a respected physician. But something strange has been happening these past days. Suddenly I came to see my selfishness and what a sinner I was. I decided to see my pastor who—would you believe it—agreed that I was a sinner and needed to be saved.

"Well, dear brother, I have good news for you. I have trusted Christ, and I want to thank you for sending that wonderful book and for your prayers that have changed my life."

When I visited that church near Atlanta some months after this, the doctor came and personally told me this story. He was excited to explain the remarkable change in his sister, but he was embarrassed to tell me THE REST OF THE STORY. In his haste to mail a book to his sister, he had sent THE WRONG BOOK, not the one he intended. He had mailed his personal copy to her—with all his requests at the close of each story! He had intended to send her a new copy. Then he smiled as he testified, "Maybe the wrong copy was the right copy—a mistake ordained by God for His door of opportunity."

I thought you might enjoy this backstage chatter. Through the many years of writing books, God has often given words of encouragement; and WE DO THANK HIM—and you for your partnership.

OTHER BOOKS BY DEVERN FROMKE

Life's Ultimate Privilege

This fifteen day journey has become a favorite. Many churches and study groups have used these lessons to stimulate personal and corporate growth. Now over 210,000 copies in a short time demonstrate both the challenge and value of this devotional book.

The Larger Window

This selection of 100 amazing stories will demonstrate how God can move each of us from being objects of grace, mercy and peace to BECOME channels and models to bless others. While the stories are both entertaining and challenging, the author has one definite goal: to move each of us from our preoccupation with what we can get from God to what He will get as we become wholly alive unto Him for fulfilling His purpose.

The Ultimate Intention

This classic has been revised with a study guide for those who desire class participation. For more than 40 years DeVern Fromke's writings have emphasized the God-centered view of reality as imperative for our vision and growth. It is no exaggeration to say that this volume has radically altered the ministry of many key leaders in this country and around the world. Now over 200,000 copies and in many languages, this volume will move every reader from a self-center to God-centeredness.

Unto Full Stature

This newly revised volume unveils very practical outworking of the Ultimate truth. The author attempts to lead each one step by step through eight levels or phases of our natural and spiritual maturity. He exposes hidden reasons why the child of God flounders in spiritual perspective, often disregards the place of the will and too often abuses his body as he zealously lives at exhaustion point. Many churches have used this with classroom participation.

I am grateful for their help:

...to Steve Cannon for designing the covers,
...to DeVon for servicing our computers,
...to Michele Captain: I have always wanted a daughter. Now the Lord
   has given one who is diligent and devoted and discerning.
...my wife, Ruth—who is God's Gracious Gift to me. Always helpful—
   discerning exactly what needs to be done.
...I give my thanks...but even more importantly:
   THE LORD IS PLEASED WITH YOUR LABOR.